W9-CIK-851

The Essence of
RALPH WALDO EMERSON

the Sage from Concord

*Compiled by Virginia Hanson
and Clarence Pedersen*

*This publication made possible with
the assistance of the Kern Foundation*

**The Theosophical Publishing House
Wheaton, Ill. U.S.A.
Madras, India / London, England**

© Copyright The Theosophical Publishing House 1985

A Quest original. All rights reserved

Second Printing 1987

A publication of the Theosophical Publishing House,
a department of the Theosophical Society in America.

Library of Congress Cataloging in Publication Data

Emerson, Ralph Waldo, 1803-1882.
  The sage from Concord.

"A Quest original"—verso t.p.
  1. Emerson, Ralph Waldo, 1803-1882—Quotations.
2. Theosophy—Quotations, maxims, etc.   I. Hanson,
Virginia.   II. Pedersen, Clarence, 1917-   III. Title.
PS1603.H34   1985   814'.3   84-40510
ISBN 0-8356-0593-0 (pbk.)

Printed in the United States of America

THE SAGE FROM CONCORD

Cover Art by *Jane A. Evans*

Contents

Contents

Foreword

As a nation, the United States had been in existence for barely a quarter of a century when Ralph Waldo Emerson was born in May of 1803. Vigorous in its youth and dedicated to the principles of freedom and equality, this new nation had still to win the wisdom of perspective and a seasoned understanding. It had set forth its goals, and to some extent its philosophy, in the Declaration of Independence and a daring new kind of Constitution. But the dynamic stroke of history which had been evoked had need of another voice—one which could give expression to the spiritual realities which might so easily have been lost sight of in the clamor of deeply sincere but conflicting views as to the best means of insuring the nation's continuance.

It was Emerson's destiny to become in some measure that voice: he spoke at once to heart and mind, with common sense made luminous by philosophic incandescence. Called by some a "practical mystic" and a "mystical pragmatist," he made explicit not only the relation between but also the actual identity of spiritual truth and human significance. His unfailing optimism, his unfaltering conviction of "the divine sufficiency of the individual," and the unceasing outpouring of his ideas in prose and poetry secured his stature as a sage and prophet in the spiritual life of the New World and established him as a key figure in the development of its culture. Volumes have since been written about Ralph Waldo Emerson, and the living quality of his contribution is apparent in the high place he continues to occupy in the esteem of thinking people more than a century after his time.

What could be more fitting than for Emerson to have appeared in New England, and specifically Boston, at the very heart of an intellectual ferment beginning to seek an instrument of release?

The early life of this rather frail youth was one of stern Christian disciplines: spelling and prayers before breakfast, daily Bible reading, Latin study, evening devotions filled his days and consumed his energies. All were designed to prepare him to carry on the family tradition of a career in the clergy—a career which he abandoned in his twenty-sixth year because he could not conform to the requirements of traditional and orthodox religion. He thought it unwise, because unnatural, to belong to any religious party; he maintained that the Bible does not direct us to become Unitarian, Presbyterian, Episcopalian, or to wear any other religious label. "When a man awakes by actual communion to the faith that God is in him, will he need any temple, any prayer?" he asked. When, later, he wrote his famous essay on "Compensation," he confessed that he had wanted to write it ever since he was a boy. "For it seemed to me when I was very young," he said, "that on this subject life was ahead of theology and the people knew more than the preachers taught."

Before the modern Theosophical Movement was born, Emerson was one of a genuine line of seers who kept alive the wisdom tradition now known as Theosophy. A life-long friendship with Thomas Carlyle, the British man of letters, accelerated the flowering of his philosophy and brought him in touch with many distinguished thinkers. Mystical Indian literature and philosophy, such as *The Bhagavad Gita* and the *Upanishads,* spoke directly to his deeply intuitive nature. Plato and Plotinus, Hegel, Shelling, and Goethe, as well as the mystical doctrines of Swedenborg, all found echoes in his own innate convictions. His motto, "Trust thyself," became the code of a remarkable group of individuals known as the New England Transcendentalists, by whom he was surrounded and of whom he was the guiding spirit.

Transcendentalism, an informal movement espoused by the most brilliant members of the New England literary community, gave a profound impetus to the intellectual and spiritual life of the vigorous new country, without which it would, to this day, be impoverished. In a very real sense, it may be said to have helped prepare the way for a wider acceptance of the philosophy which found its focus in the establishment of the Theosophical Society in the late nineteenth century and which now has spread not only throughout this country but over the entire world.

It is true that rigid structure and form are not the chief characteristics of Emerson's literary style; his prose often has a strongly poetic quality, while his poetry has sometimes been called "harsh and didactic." He spoke of himself as a "husky singer." The strongest mark of that intuition, which refused to be bound by predetermined rules, is found in the swift, flashing, epigrammatic sentence embodying a truth which strikes inward to the heart. Custom and consistency never earned his homage. "The books which once we valued as the apple of our eyes, we have quite exhausted," he commented. "What is that but saying that we have come up with the point of view which the Universal Mind took through the eyes of one scribe? We have been that man and passed on."

The compilers of this small book of gems from the pen of this great theosophical transcendentalist have selected passages which will, for a long time to come, call us to move forward to greater freedom, greater understanding, greater use of the gifts which are ours by virtue of being human. "We lie in the lap of immense intelligence," Emerson assures us, "which makes us receivers of its truth and

Foreword

organs of its activity. When we discern justice, when we discern truth, we do nothing of ourselves but allow a passage to its beams." This distillation of the essence of Emerson aspires in some measure to facilitate that passage for today's seeker who must read as he runs.

VIRGINIA HANSON

From "History"

There is no great and no small
To the Soul that maketh all:
And where it cometh, all things are;
And it cometh everywhere.

I am owner of the sphere,
Of the seven stars and the solar year,
Of Caesar's hand, and Plato's brain,
Of Lord Christ's heart, and Shakespeare's
  strain.

— R E W —

There is one mind common to all individual
men....Who hath access to this universal

mind is a party to all that is or can be done, for this is the only and sovereign agent.

— ℛ℮𝒲 —

...the thought is always prior to the fact; all the facts of history pre-exist in the mind as laws.

— ℛ℮𝒲 —

...all that is said of the wise man by Stoic or Oriental or modern essayist, describes to each reader his own idea, describes his unattained but attainable self.

— ℛ℮𝒲 —

All history becomes subjective; in other words there is properly no history, only biography. Every mind must know the whole lesson for itself—must go over the whole ground. What it does not see, what it does not live, it will not know.

To the poet, to the philosopher, to the saint, all things are friendly and sacred, all events profitable, all days holy, all men divine. For the eye is fastened on the life, and slights the circumstance. Every chemical substance, every plant, every animal in its growth, teaches the unity of cause, the variety of appearance.

Nature is a mutable cloud which is always and never the same....Nothing is so fleeting as form; yet never does it quite deny itself.

3

— R*E*W —

The Gothic cathedral is a blossoming in stone subdued by the insatiable demand of harmony in man.

— R*E*W —

Everything the individual sees without him corresponds to his states of mind, and every thing is in turn intelligible to him, as his on-ward thinking leads him into the truth to which that fact or series belongs.

— R*E*W —

...the poet was no odd fellow who described strange and impossible situations, but that universal man wrote by his pen a confession true for one and true for all.

No man can antedate his experience, or guess what faculty or feeling a new object shall unlock, any more than he can draw today the face of a person whom he shall see tomorrow for the first time.

From "Self-Reliance"

Man is his own star; and the soul that can
Render an honest and a perfect man,
Commands all light, all influence, all fate;
Nothing to him falls early or too late.
Our acts our angels are, or good or ill,
Our fatal shadows that walk by us still.

— REW —

To believe your own thought, to believe that
what is true for you in your private heart is
true for all men—that is genius.

— REW —

From "Self-Reliance"

A man should learn to detect and watch that gleam of light which flashes across his mind from within, more than the lustre of the firmament of bards and sages.

— *RℰW* —

There is a time in every man's education when he arrives at the conviction that envy is ignorance; that imitation is suicide; that he must take himself for better for worse as his portion; that though the wide universe is full of good, no kernel of nourishing corn can come to him but through his toil bestowed on that plot of ground which is given to him to till.

— *RℰW* —

We but half express ourselves, and are ashamed of that divine idea which each of us represents.... Trust thyself: every heart vibrates to that iron string.

7

— R&W —

Nothing is at last sacred but the integrity of your own mind.

— R&W —

What I must do is all that concerns me, not what the people think. This rule, equally arduous in actual and in intellectual life, may serve for the whole distinction between greatness and meanness.

— R&W —

It is easy in the world to live after the world's opinions; it is easy in solitude to live after our own; but the great man is he who in the midst of the crowd keeps with perfect sweetness the independence of solitude.

— R&W —

A foolish consistency is the hobgoblin of little minds.... With consistency a great soul has simply nothing to do. He may as well concern himself with his shadow on the wall. Speak what you think now in hard words and tomorrow speak what tomorrow thinks in hard words again, though it contradict everything you said today.

— *R E W* —

We pass for what we are. Character teaches above our wills. Men imagine that they communicate their virtue or vice only by overt actions, and do not see that virtue or vice emits a breath every morning.

— *R E W* —

Greatness appeals to the future.... Be it how it will, do right now. Always scorn appearances and you always may. The force of character is cumulative.

— RℰW —

. . . there is a great responsible Thinker and Actor working wherever a man works; that a true man belongs to no other time or place, but is the center of things.

— RℰW —

. . . that Source, at once the essence of genius, of virtue, and of life, which we call Spontaneity or Instinct. We denote this primary wisdom as Intuition, whilst all later teachings are tuitions. In that deep force, the last fact behind which analysis cannot go, all things find their common origin.

— RℰW —

We lie in the lap of immense intelligence, which makes us receivers of its truth and organs of its activity.

Every man discriminates between the voluntary acts of his mind and his involuntary perceptions, and knows that to his involuntary perceptions a perfect faith is due.

If we live truly, we shall see truly. It is as easy for the strong man to be strong, as it is for the weak to be weak.

In the hour of vision there is nothing that can be called gratitude, nor properly joy. The soul raised over passion beholds identity and eternal causation, perceives the self-existence of Truth and Right, and calms itself with knowing that all things go well.

— *R E W* —

Life only avails, not the having lived.

— *R E W* —

I will so trust that what is deep is holy, that I will do strongly before the sun and moon whatever inly rejoices me and the heart appoints.

— *R E W* —

And truly it demands something godlike in him who has cast off the common motives of humanity and has ventured to trust himself for a taskmaster.

— ℛℰ𝒲 —

Prayer that craves a particular commodity, anything less than all good, is vicious. . . . As soon as the man is at one with God, he will not beg. He will then see prayer in all action.

— ℛℰ𝒲 —

Discontent is the want of self-reliance; it is infirmity of will. Regret calamities if you can thereby help the sufferer; if not, attend your own work and already the evil begins to be repaired.

— ℛℰ𝒲 —

Insist on yourself; never imitate. Your own gift you can present every moment with the cumulative force of a whole life's cultivation; but of the adopted talent of another you have only an extemporaneous half possession.

The Sage from Concord

— R E W —

It is only as a man puts off all foreign support and stands alone that I see him to be strong and to prevail.

— R E W —

Nothing can bring you peace but yourself. Nothing can bring you peace but the triumph of principles.

From "Compensation"

I think that our popular theology has gained in decorum, and not in principle, over the superstitions it has displaced. But men are better than their theology. Their daily life gives it the lie. Every ingenuous and aspiring soul leaves the doctrine behind him in his own experience.

— R E W —

Every excess causes a defect; every defect an excess. Every sweet hath its sour; every evil its good. Every faculty which is a receiver of pleasure has an equal penalty put on its abuse. It is to answer for its moderation with its life.

— R E W —

...the universe is represented in every one of its particles. Every thing in nature contains all the powers of nature. Every thing is made of one hidden stuff.

— R E W —

What we call retribution is the universal necessity by which the whole appears wherever a part appears.

— R E W —

Cause and effect, means and ends, seed and fruit, cannot be severed; for the effect already blooms in the cause, the end pre-exists in the means, the fruit in the seed.

— R E W —

From "Compensation"

Proverbs, like the sacred books of each nation,
are the sanctuary of the intuitions. That which
the droning world, chained to appearances,
will not allow the realist to say in his own
words, it will suffer him to say in proverbs
without contradiction.

— *RE W* —

Fear is an instructor of great sagacity and the
herald of all revolutions. One thing he teaches,
that there is rottenness where he appears. He
is a carrion crow, and though you see not well
what he hovers for, there is death somewhere.

— *RE W* —

...pay every just demand on your time, your
talents, or your heart. Always pay; for first or
last you must pay your entire debt.

— *RE W* —

The law of nature is, Do the thing, and you shall have the power; but they who do not the thing have not the power.

— R E W —

The good man has absolute good, which like fire turns every thing to its own nature, so that you cannot do him any harm.

— R E W —

As every man had ever a point of pride that was not injurious to him, so no man had ever a defect that was not somewhere made useful to him.... Every man in his lifetime needs to thank his faults.

— R E W —

In general, every evil to which we do not succumb is a benefactor.

18

From "Compensation"

— ℛℰ𝒲 —

It is as impossible for man to be cheated by anyone but himself, as for a thing to be and not to be at the same time. There is a third silent party to all our bargains. The nature and soul of things takes on itself the guaranty of the fulfillment of every contract, so that honest service cannot come to loss.

— ℛℰ𝒲 —

There is a deeper fact in the soul than compensation, to wit, its own nature. The soul is not a compensation, but a life. The soul *is*. Under all this running sea of circumstance, whose waters ebb and flow with perfect balance, lies the aboriginal abyss of real Being....Being is the vast affirmative.

— ℛℰ𝒲 —

19

There can be no excess to love, none to knowledge, none to beauty, when these attributes are considered in the purest sense. The soul refuses limits and always affirms an Optimism, never a Pessimism.

— *REW* —

Such should be the outward biography of man in time, a putting off of dead circumstances day by day, as he renews his raiment day by day.

— *REW* —

The sure years reveal the deep remedial force that underlies all facts.

Brahma

BRAHMA

If the red slayer think he slays,
  Or if the slain think he is slain,
They know not well the subtle ways
  I keep, and pass, and turn again.

Far or forgot to me is near;
  Shadow and sunlight are the same;
The vanished gods to me appear;
  And one to me are shame and fame.

They reckon ill who leave me out;
  When me they fly, I am the wings;
I am the doubter and the doubt,
  And I the hymn the Brahmin sings.

The strong gods pine for my abode,
  And pine in vain the sacred Seven;
But thou, meek lover of the good!
  Find me, and turn thy back on heaven.

From "Spiritual Laws"

When the act of reflection takes place in the mind, when we look at ourselves in the light of thought, we discover that our life is embosomed in beauty. . . . The soul will not know either deformity or pain. . . . All loss, all pain, is particular; the universe remains at heart unhurt.

— *RℰW* —

The less a man thinks or knows about his virtues the better we like him.

— *RℰW* —

We miscreate our own evils. We interfere with the optimism of nature...we are begirt with laws which execute themselves.

— R𝓔W —

It is natural and beautiful that childhood should inquire and maturity should teach; but it is time enough to answer questions when they are asked.

— R𝓔W —

We judge a man's wisdom by his hope, knowing that the perception of the inexhaustibleness of nature is an immortal youth.

— R𝓔W —

A little consideration of what takes place around us every day would show us that a higher law than that of our will regulates events; that our painful labors are unnecessary and fruitless; that only in our easy, simple, spontaneous action are we strong.

— R E W —

There is a soul at the center of nature and over the will of every man, so that none of us can wrong the universe.

— R E W —

Each man has his own vocation. The talent is the call. There is one direction in which all space is open to him. He has faculties silently inviting him thither to endless exertion.

— R E W —

Every man has this call of the power to do somewhat unique, and no man has any other call.

24

From "Spiritual Laws"

— RℰW —

What a man does, that he has. What has he to do with hope or fear? In himself is his might. Let him regard no good as solid but that which is in his nature and which must grow out of him as long as he exists.

— RℰW —

A man is a method, a progressive arrangement; a selecting principle, gathering his like to him wherever he goes.

— RℰW —

What your heart thinks great, is great. The soul's emphasis is always right.

— RℰW —

God screens us evermore from premature ideas. Our eyes are holden that we cannot see

25

things that stare us in the face, until the hour arrives when the mind is ripened; then we behold them, and the time when we saw them not is like a dream.

— R E W —

There is no teaching until the pupil is brought into the same state or principle in which you are; a transfusion takes place; he is you and you are he; then is a teaching, and by no unfriendly chance or bad company can he ever quite lose the benefit.

— R E W —

The way to speak and write what shall not go out of fashion is to speak and write sincerely....He that writes to himself writes to an eternal public.

— ℛℰ𝒲 —

Human character evermore publishes itself.
The most fugitive deed and word, the mere air
of doing a thing, the intimated purpose, ex-
presses character. If you act you show character; if you sit still, if you sleep, you show it.

— ℛℰ𝒲 —

That which we do not believe we cannot ade-
quately say, though we may repeat the words
never so often.

— ℛℰ𝒲 —

As much virtue as there is, so much appears;
as much goodness as there is, so much rever-
ence it commands. All the devils respect virtue. The high, the generous, the self-devoted
sect will always instruct and command

mankind. Never was a sincere word utterly lost. Never a magnanimity fell to the ground but there was some heart to greet and accept it unexpectedly.

— R E W —

Virtue is the adherence in action to the nature of things and the nature of things makes it prevalent. It consists in a perpetual substitution of being for seeming, and with sublime propriety God is described as saying, I AM.

— R E W —

Real action is in silent moments. The epochs of our life are not in the visible facts of our choice of a calling, our marriage, our acquisition of an office, and the like, but in a silent thought by the wayside as we walk.

— R E W —

The fact that I am here certainly shows me that the soul had need of an organ here.

Only that soul can be my friend which I encounter on the line of my own march, that soul to which I do not decline and which does not decline to me, but, native of the same celestial latitude, repeats in its own all my experience.

Over all things that are agreeable to his nature and genius the man has the highest right. Everywhere he may take what belongs to his spiritual estate, nor can he take anything else though all doors were open, nor can all the force of men hinder him from taking so much.

From "Love"

Every promise of the soul has innumerable fulfillments; each of its joys ripens into a new want.

— REW —

For persons are love's world, and the coldest philosopher cannot recount the debt of the young soul wandering here in nature to the power of love, without being tempted to unsay, as treasonable to nature, aught derogatory to the social instincts.

— REW —

From "Love"

By conversation with that which is in itself excellent, magnanimous, lowly, and just, the lover comes to a warmer love of these nobilities, and a quicker apprehension of them.

— *RℰW* —

It is the nature and end of this relation that they should represent the human race to each other.

— *RℰW* —

...the purification of the intellect and the heart from year to year is the real marriage, foreseen and prepared from the first, and wholly above their consciousness.

— *RℰW* —

We are put in training for a love which knows not sex, nor person, nor partiality, but which

31

seeks virtue and wisdom everywhere, to the end of increasing virtue and wisdom. We are by nature observers, and thereby learners.

FORBEARANCE

Hast thou named all the birds without a
   gun?
Loved the wood-rose, and left it on its stalk?
At rich men's tables eaten bread and pulse?
Unarmed, faced danger with a heart of trust?
And loved so well a high behavior
In man or maid, that thou from speech
   refrained,
Nobility more nobly to repay?
O, be my friend, and teach me to be thine!

From "Friendship"

We have a great deal more kindness than is ever spoken...the whole human family is bathed with an element of love like a fine ether.

— R E W —

Let the soul be assured that somewhere in the universe it should rejoin its friend, and it would be content and cheerful alone for a thousand years.

— R E W —

From "Friendship"

I must feel pride in my friend's accomplishments as if they were mine, and a property in his virtues.

— R E W —

Our friendships hurry to short and poor conclusions, because we have made them a texture of wine and dreams, instead of the tough fibre of the human heart. The laws of friendship are austere and eternal, of one web with the laws of nature and of morals.

— R E W —

For now, after so many ages of experience, what do we know of nature or of ourselves? Not one step has man taken towards the solution of the problem of his destiny.

— R E W —

Happy is the house that shelters a friend!

— R E W —

Leave to the diamond its ages to grow, nor expect to accelerate the births of the eternal. Friendship demands a religious treatment. We talk of choosing our friends, but friends are self-elected.

— R E W —

There can never be deep peace between two spirits, never mutual respect, until in their dialogue each stands for the whole world.

— R E W —

What is so great as friendship, let us carry with what grandeur of spirit we can. Let us be silent—so we may hear the whisper of the gods. . . . Wait and thy heart shall speak.

36

From "Friendship"

— R E W —

It is foolish to be afraid of making our ties too
spiritual as if so we could lose any genuine
love.

From "Prudence"

Prudence does not go behind nature and ask whence it is. It takes the laws of the world whereby man's being is conditioned, as they are, and keeps these laws that it may enjoy their proper good.

— *R℮W* —

Some wisdom comes out of every natural and innocent action.

— *R℮W* —

If you believe in the soul, do not clutch at sensual sweetness before it is ripe on the slow tree of cause and effect.

From "Prudence"

— R&W —

Is it not better that a man should accept the first pains and mortifications...which nature is not slack in sending him, as hints that he must expect no other good than the just fruit of his own labor and self-denial?

— R&W —

As much wisdom may be expended on a private economy as on an empire, and as much wisdom may be drawn from it.

— R&W —

We must not try to write the laws of any one virtue, looking at that only. Human nature loves no contradictions, but is symmetrical.

— R&W —

In regard to disagreeable and formidable things, prudence does not consist in evasion or in flight, but in courage.

We refuse sympathy and intimacy with people, as if we waited for some better sympathy and intimacy to come. But whence and when? Tomorrow will be like today. Life wastes itself whilst we are preparing to live.

From "Heroism"

"Paradise is under the shadow of swords."
                                    Mahomet

Ruby wine is drunk by knaves,
Sugar spends to fatten slaves,
Rose and vine-leaf deck buffoons;
Thunderclouds are Jove's festoons,
Drooping oft in wreaths of dread
Lightning-knotted round his head:
The hero is not fed on sweets,
Daily his own heart he eats;
Chambers of the great are jails,
And head-winds right for royal sails.

— R E W —

The violations of the laws of nature by our predecessors and our contemporaries are punished in us also.

— *R E W* —

Self-trust is the essence of heroism. It is the state of the soul at war, and its ultimate objects are the last defiance of falsehood and wrong, and the power to bear all that can be inflicted by evil agents.

— *R E W* —

The magnanimous know very well that they who give time, or money, or shelter, to the stranger—so it be done for love and not for ostentation—do, as it were, put God under obligation to them, so perfect are the compensations of the universe.

 — *R E W* —

The heroic soul does not sell its justice and its nobleness. It does not ask to dine nicely and to sleep warm. The essence of greatness is the perception that virtue is enough.

— *R E W* —

The characteristic of heroism is its persistency. All men have wandering impulses, fits and starts of generosity. But when you have chosen your part, abide by it, and do not weakly try to reconcile yourself with the world. The heroic cannot be common, nor the common the heroic.

WOODNOTES

3

The timid it concerns to ask their way,
And fear what foe in caves and swamps can
  stray,
To make no step until the event is known,
And ills to come as evils past bemoan.
Not so the wise; no coward watch he keeps
To spy what danger on his pathway creeps;
Go where he will, the wise man is at home,
His hearth the earth,—his hall the azure
  dome;
Where his clear spirit leads him, there's his
  road
By God's own light illumined and foreshowed.

From "The Over-Soul"

Our faith comes in moments; our vice is habitual. Yet there is a depth in those brief moments which constrains us to ascribe more reality to them than to all other experiences.

We grant that human life is mean, but how did we find out that it was mean? What is the ground of this uneasiness of ours; of this odd discontent? What is the universal sense of want and ignorance but the fine innuendo by which the soul makes its enormous claim?

45

Man is a stream whose source is hidden.

— R E W —

I am constrained every moment to acknowledge a higher origin for events than the will I call mine.

— R E W —

We live in succession, in division, in parts, in particles. Meantime within man is the soul of the whole; the wise silence; the universal beauty, to which every part and particle is equally related; the eternal One.

— R E W —

We see the world piece by piece, as the sun, the moon, the animal, the tree; but the whole, of which these are the shining parts, is the Soul.

— ℛℰ𝒲 —

All goes to show that the soul of man is not an organ, but animates and exercises all the organs; is not a function, like the power of memory, of calculation, of comparison, but uses these as hands and feet.

— ℛℰ𝒲 —

A man is the facade of a temple wherein all wisdom and all good abide.

— ℛℰ𝒲 —

The blindness of the intellect begins when it would be something of itself.

— ℛℰ𝒲 —

As there is no screen or ceiling between our heads and the infinite heavens, so is there no bar or wall in the soul, where man, the effect, ceases, and God, the cause, begins.

— ℛℰ𝒲 —

The soul looketh steadily forwards, creating a world before her, leaving worlds behind her. She has no dates, nor rites, nor persons, nor specialties, nor men. The soul knows only the soul; the web of events is the flowing robe in which she is clothed.

— ℛℰ𝒲 —

The heart which abandons itself to the Supreme Mind finds itself related to all its works, and will travel a royal road to particular knowledges and powers.

— ℛℰ𝒲 —

From "The Over-Soul"

The soul requires purity, but purity is not it; requires justice, but justice is not that; requires beneficence, but is somewhat better.

The soul is the perceiver and revealer of truth. We know truth when we see it, let skeptic and scoffer say what they choose.

We are wiser than we know. If we will not interfere with our thought, but will act entirely, or see how the thing stands in God, we know the particular thing, and every thing, and every man. For the Maker of all things and all persons stands behind us and casts his dread omniscience through us over things.

A thrill passes through all men at the reception of new truth, or at the performance of a great action, which comes out of the heart of nature.

— R E W —

The soul answers never by words, but by the thing itself that is inquired after.

— R E W —

It is not in an arbitrary "decree of God" but in the nature of man, that a veil shuts down on the facts of tomorrow; for the soul will not have us read any other cipher than that of cause and effect.

— R E W —

That which we are, we shall teach, not voluntarily but involuntarily.

From "The Over-Soul"

— R E W —

It is no use to preach to me from without. I can do that too easily myself.

— R E W —

But if a man do not speak from within the veil, where the word is one with that it tells of, let him lowly confess it.

— R E W —

But genius is religious. It is a larger imbibing of the common heart. It is not anomalous, but more like and not less like other men.

— R E W —

The soul is superior to its knowledge, wiser than any of its works.

— ℛℰ𝒲 —

It comes to the lowly and simple; it comes to whosoever will put off what is foreign and proud; it comes as insight; it comes as serenity and grandeur.

— ℛℰ𝒲 —

Ineffable is the union of man and God in every act of the soul. The simplest person who in his integrity worships God, becomes God; yet for ever and ever the influx of this better and universal self is new and unsearchable. It inspires awe and astonishment.

— ℛℰ𝒲 —

When we have broken our god of tradition and ceased from our god of rhetoric, then may God fore the heart with his presence.

From "The Over-Soul"

— R E W —

The things that are really for thee gravitate to thee.

— R E W —

O believe, as thou livest, that every sound that is spoken over the round world, which thou oughtest to hear, will vibrate to thine ear. Every proverb, every book, every byword that belongs to thee for aid or comfort, shall surely come home through open or winding passages.

— R E W —

Every friend whom not thy fantastic will but the great and tender heart in thee craveth, shall lock thee in his embrace. And this because the heart in thee is the heart of all; not a valve, not a wall, not an intersection is there

anywhere in nature, but one blood rolls un-
interruptedly an endless circulation through
all men, as the water of the globe is all one sea,
and, truly seen, its tide is one.

— *REW* —

He that finds God a sweet enveloping thought
to him never counts his company.

— *REW* —

The faith that stands on authority is not faith.
The reliance on authority measures the decline
of religion, the withdrawal of the soul.

— *REW* —

The soul gives itself, alone, original, and pure,
to the Lonely, Original and Pure, who, on that
condition, gladly inhabits, leads and speaks
through it.

54

— ℛ𝓔𝓦 —

Thus revering the soul, and learning, as the ancient said, that "its beauty is immense," man will come to see that the world is the perennial miracle which the soul worketh, and be less astonished at particular wonders; he will learn that there is no profane history; that all history is sacred; that the universe is represented in an atom, in a moment of time. He will weave no longer a spotted life of shreds and patches, but he will live with a divine unity. He will cease from what is base and frivolous in his life and be content with all places and with any service he can render. He will calmly front the morrow in the negligency of that trust which carries God with it and so hath already the whole future in the bottom of the heart.

NATURE

1

A subtle chain of countless rings
The next unto the farthest brings;
The eye reads omens where it goes,
And speaks all languages the rose;
And, striving to be man, the worm
Mounts through all the spires of form.

From "Circles"

Our life is an apprenticeship to the truth that around every circle another can be drawn; that there is no end in nature, but every end is a beginning.

— *R E W* —

Every ultimate fact is only the first of a new series. Every general law only a particular fact of some more general law presently to disclose itself.

— *R E W* —

Every man supposes himself not to be fully understood.... The last chamber, the last

57

closet, he must feel was never opened; there is always a residuum unknown, unanalyzable. That is, every man believes that he has a greater possibility.

— R E W —

There are degrees in idealism. We learn first to play with it academically, as the magnet was once a toy. Then we see in the heyday of youth and poetry that it may be true, that it is true in gleams and fragments. Then its countenance waxes stern and grand, and we see that it must be true.

— R E W —

Good as is discourse, silence is better, and shames it. The length of the discourse indicates the distance of thought betwixt the speaker and the hearer. If they were at a perfect understanding in any part, no words would be necessary thereon.

— ℛℰ𝒲 —

In nature every moment is new; the past is always swallowed and forgotten; the coming only is sacred. Nothing is secure but life, transition, the energizing spirit.

— ℛℰ𝒲 —

People wish to be settled; only as far as they are unsettled is there any hope for them.

— ℛℰ𝒲 —

The difference between talents and character is adroitness to keep the old and trodden round, and power and courage to make a new road to new and better goals.

The Sage from Concord

— R E W —

The one thing which we seek with insatiable desire is to forget ourselves, to be surprised out of our propriety, to lose our sempiternal memory and do something without knowing how or why; in short, to draw a new circle. Nothing great was ever achieved without enthusiasm. The way of life is wonderful; it is by abandonment.

From "Intellect"

He who is immersed in what concerns person or place cannot see the problem of existence.

— R E W —

God enters by a private door into every individual.

— R E W —

Our spontaneous action is always the best. You cannot with your best deliberation and heed come so close to any question as your spontaneous glance shall bring you, whilst you rise from your bed, or walk abroad in the morning after meditating the matter before sleep on the previous night.

— ℛ𝓔𝓦 —

All our progress is an unfolding, like the vegetable bud. You have first an instinct, then an opinion, then a knowledge, as the plant has root, bud and fruit. Trust the instinct to the end.

— ℛ𝓔𝓦 —

We say, I will walk abroad, and the truth will take form and clearness to me. But we come in, and are as far from it as at first. Then, in a moment and unannounced, the truth appears. But the oracle comes because we had previously laid siege to the shrine. So now you must labor with your brains, and now you must forbear your activity and see what the great Soul showeth.

62

From "Intellect"

— R𝓔W —

Truth is our element of life, yet if a man fasten his attention on a single aspect of truth and apply himself to that alone for a long time, the truth becomes distorted and not itself but falsehood. How wearisome the grammarian, the phrenologist, the political or religious fanatic, or indeed any possessed mortal whose balance is lost by the exaggeration of a single topic.

— R𝓔W —

Neither by detachment, neither by aggregation, is the integrity of the intellect transmitted to its works. It must have the same wholeness which nature has.

— R𝓔W —

God offers to every mind its choice between truth and repose. Take which you please, —you can never have both.

— ℛℰ𝒲 —

One soul is a counterpoise of all souls, as a capillary column of water is a balance for the sea.

— ℛℰ𝒲 —

Hermes, Heraclitus, Empedocles, Plato, Plotinus, Olympiodorus, Proclus, Synesius and the rest, have somewhat so vast in their logic, so primary in their thinking, that it seems antecedent to all the ordinary distinctions of rhetoric and literature, and to be at once poetry and music and dancing and astronomy and mathematics. I am present at the sowing of the seed of the world.

The Rhodora

THE RHODORA:

On Being Asked, Whence Is the Flower?

In May, when sea-winds pierced our
solitudes,
I found the fresh Rhodora in the woods,
Spreading its leafless blooms in a damp
nook,
To please the desert and the sluggish brook.
The purple petals, fallen in the pool,
Made the black water with their beauty gay;
Here might the red-bird come his plumes to
cool,
And court the flower that cheapens his
array.
Rhodora! if the sages ask thee why
This charm is wasted on the earth and sky,
Tell them, dear, that if eyes were made for
seeing,
Then Beauty is its own excuse for being:
Why thou wert there, O rival of the rose!
I never thought to ask, I never knew:
But, in my simple ignorance, suppose
The self-same Power that brought me there
brought you.

From "Art"

Because the soul is progressive, it never quite repeats itself, but in every act attempts the production of a new and fairer whole.

— REW —

As far as the spiritual character of the period overpowers the artist and finds expression in his work, so far it will retain a certain grandeur, and will represent to future beholders the Unknown, the Inevitable, the Divine.

— REW —

Now that which is inevitable in the work has a higher charm than individual talent can ever give, inasmuch as the artist's pen or chisel seems to have been held and guided by a gigantic hand to inscribe a line in the history of the human race. This circumstance gives a value to the Egyptian hieroglyphics, to the Indian, Chinese and Mexican idols, however gross and shapeless. They denote the height of the human soul in that hour, and were not fantastic, but sprung from a necessity as deep as the world.

— *REW* —

We are immersed in beauty, but our eyes have no clear vision.

— *REW* —

The best of beauty is a finer charm than skill in surfaces, in outlines, or rules of art can ever teach, namely a radiation from the work of art, of human character.

67

— ℛℰ𝒲 —

Art is the need to create. Nothing less than the creation of man and nature is its end.

— ℛℰ𝒲 —

True art is never fixed, but always flowing. The sweetest music is not in the oratorio, but in the human voice when it speaks from its instant life tones of tenderness, truth, or courage.

— ℛℰ𝒲 —

A true announcement of the law of creation would carry art up into the kingdom of nature, and destroy its separate and contrasted existence.

From "Art"

As soon as beauty is sought, not from religion and love but for pleasure, it degrades the seeker.

In nature, all is useful, all is beautiful. It is therefore beautiful because it is alive.

From "The Poet"

The breadth of the problem is great, for the poet is representative. He stands among partial men for the complete man, and apprises us not of his wealth, but of the common-wealth.

— *R E W* —

Too feeble fall the impressions of nature on us to make us artists. Every touch should thrill.

— *R E W* —

The Universe has three children, born at one time...the Knower, the Doer, and the Sayer. These stand respectively for the love of truth,

70

for the love of good, and for the love of beauty. These three are equal.

— R E W —

Poetry was all written before time was, and whenever we are so finely organized that we can penetrate into that region where the air is music, we hear those primal warblings and attempt to write them down.

— R E W —

The experience of each new age requires a new confession, and the world seems always waiting for its poet.

— R E W —

We know that the secret of the world is profound, but who or what shall be our interpreter, we know not.

71

The Sage from Concord

— R E W —

Man, never so often deceived, still watches for the arrival of a brother who can hold him steady to a truth until he has made it his own.

— R E W —

For it is not meters, but a meter-making argument that makes a poem—a thought so passionate and alive that like the spirit of a plant or an animal it has an architecture of its own, and adorns nature with a new thing.

— R E W —

Since everything in nature answers to a moral power, if any phenomenon remains brute and dark it is because the corresponding faculty in the observer is not yet active.

From "The Poet"

— ℛℰℋ —

Nature has a higher end, in the production of new individuals, than security, namely *ascension,* or the passage of the soul into higher forms.

— ℛℰℋ —

The condition of true naming, on the poet's part, is his resigning himself to the divine *aura* which breathes through forms.

— ℛℰℋ —

It is a secret which every intellectual man quickly learns, that beyond the energy of his possessed and conscious intellect he is capable of a new energy...by abandonment to the nature of things; that beside his privacy of power as an individual man, there is a great

73

public power on which he can draw, by unlocking, at all risks, his human doors, and suffering the ethereal tides to roll and circulate through him; then he is caught up into the life of the Universe, his speech is thunder, his thought is law, and his words are universally intelligible as the plants and animals.

THE PROBLEM

4

Know'st thou what wove yon woodbird's nest
Of leaves, and feathers from her breast?
Or how the fish outbuilt her shell,
Painting with morn each annual cell?
Or how the sacred pine tree adds
To her old leaves new myriads?
Such and so grew these holy piles,
Whilst love and terror laid the tiles.
Each proudly wears the Parthenon,
As the best gem upon her zone,
And Morning opes with haste her lids
To gaze upon the Pyramids;
O'er England's abbeys bends the sky,
As on its friends, with kindred eye;
For out of Thought's interior sphere
These wonders rose to upper air;
And Nature gladly gave them place,
Adopted them into her race,
And granted them an equal date
With Andes and with Ararat.

From "Experience"

So much of our time is preparation, so much is routine, and so much retrospect, that the pith of each man's genius contracts itself to a very few hours.

— R E W —

The only thing grief has taught me is to know how shallow it is. That, like all the rest, plays about the surface, and never introduces me into the reality, for contact with which we would even pay the costly price of sons and lovers.

— R E W —

From "Experience"

Spirit is matter reduced to an extreme thinness: O *so* thin!—But the definition of *spiritual* should be, *that which is its own evidence.*

—R̃Ẽ𝒲—

Into every intelligence there is a door which is never closed, through which the creator passes.

—R̃Ẽ𝒲—

A man is like a bit of Labrador spar, which has no luster as you turn it in your hand until you come to a particular angle; then it shows deep and beautiful colors.

—R̃Ẽ𝒲—

Like a bird which alights nowhere, but hops perpetually from bough to bough, is the Power which abides in no man and no woman, but for a moment speaks from this one, and for another moment from that one.

— ℛℰ𝒲 —

To finish the moment, to find the journey's end in every step of the road, to live the greatest number of good hours, is wisdom.

— ℛℰ𝒲 —

I settle myself ever the firmer in the creed that we should not postpone and refer and wish, but do broad justice where we are, by whomsoever we deal with, accepting our actual companions and circumstances, however humble or odious, as whole pleasure for us.

— ℛℰ𝒲 —

Human life is made up of the two elements, power and form, and the proportion must be invariably kept if we would have it sweet and sound. Each of these elements in excess makes a mischief as hurtful as its defect....every good quality is noxious if unmixed.

— *R E W* —

A man is a golden impossibility. The line he must walk is a hair's breadth. The wise through excess of wisdom is made a fool.

— *R E W* —

Life is a series of surprises, and would not be worth taking or keeping if it were not. God delights to isolate us every day, and hide from us the past and the future.

— *R E W* —

The results of life are uncalculated and un-calculable. The years teach much which the days never know.

— ℛℰ𝒲 —

The consciousness in each man is a sliding scale, which identifies him now with the First Cause, and now with the flesh of his body; life above life, in infinite degrees.

— ℛℰ𝒲 —

It is not what we believe concerning the immortality of the soul or the like, but *the universal impulse to believe,* that is the material circumstance and is the principal fact in the history of the globe.

— ℛℰ𝒲 —

The spirit is not helpless or needful of mediate organs. It has plentiful powers and direct effects. I am explained without explaining, I am felt without acting, and where I am not.

From "Experience"

— ℛℰ𝒲 —

In liberated moments we know that a new picture of life and duty is already possible; the elements already exist in many minds around you of a doctrine of life which shall transcend any written record we have.

— ℛℰ𝒲 —

Life will be imaged, but cannot be divided nor doubled. Any invasion of its unity would be chaos.

— ℛℰ𝒲 —

As I am, so I see; use what language we will, we can never say anything but what we are.

— ℛℰ𝒲 —

We dress our garden, eat our dinners, discuss the household with our wives, and these things make no impression, are forgotten next week; but, in the solitude to which every man is always returning, he has a sanity and revelations which in his passage into new worlds he will carry with him.

Seashore

SEASHORE

2   *Behold the Sea,*
The opaline, the plentiful and strong,
Yet beautiful as is the rose in June,
Fresh as the trickling rainbow of July;
Sea full of food, the nourisher of kinds,
Purger of earth, and medicine of men;
Creating a sweet climate by my breath,
Washing out harms and griefs from memory,
And, in my mathematic ebb and flow,
Giving a hint of that which changes not.
Rich are the sea-gods:—who gives gifts but
   they?
They grope the sea for pearls, but more than
   pearls:
They pluck Force thence, and give it to the
   wise.
For every wave is wealth to Daedalus,
Wealth to the cunning artist who can work
This matchless strength. Where shall he
   find, O waves!
A load your Atlas shoulders cannot lift?

83

From "Character"

...men of character are the conscience of the society to which they belong.

— REW —

Everything in nature is bipolar, or has a positive and a negative pole....Spirit is the positive, the event is the negative.... Character may be ranked as having its natural place in the north. It shares the magnetic currents of the system.

— REW —

From "Character"

We boast our emancipation from many superstitions; but if we have broken any idols it is through a transfer of idolatry.

— R E W —

It is not enough that the intellect should see the evils and their remedy. We shall still postpone our existence, nor take the ground to which we are entitled, whilst it is only a thought and not a spirit that incites us.

— R E W —

Character is nature in its highest form. It is of no use to ape it or to contend with it.

— R E W —

This masterpiece is best where no hands but nature's have been laid on it.

— ℛ𝓔𝓦 —

He is a dull observer whose experience has not
taught him the reality and force of magic, as
well as of chemistry. The coldest precision
cannot go abroad without encountering
inexplicable influences.

— ℛ𝓔𝓦 —

Is there any religion but this, to know that
wherever in the wide desert of being the holy
sentiment we cherish has opened into a flower,
it blooms for me? If none sees it, I see it; I am
aware, if I alone, of the greatness of the fact.

From "Manners"

...personal force never goes out of fashion. That is still paramount today, and in the moving crowd of good society the men of valor and reality are known and rise to their natural place.

— *RℰW* —

Moral qualities rule the world, but at short distances the senses are despotic.

— *RℰW* —

The love of beauty is mainly the love of measure or proportion. The person who screams, or uses the superlative degree, or converses with heat, puts whole drawing-rooms to flight. If you wish to be loved, love measure.

— R E W —

A man is but a little thing in the midst of the objects of nature, yet, by the moral quality radiating from his countenance he may abolish all considerations of magnitude, and in his manners equal the majesty of the world.

— R E W —

Everything that is called fashion and courtesy humbles itself before the cause and fountain of honor, creator of titles and dignities, namely the heart of love.

— R E W —

Without the rich heart, wealth is an ugly beggar.

—RЄW—

It is easy to see that what is called by distinction society and fashion has good laws as well as bad, has much that is necessary, and much that is absurd. Too good for banning, and too bad for blessing.

From "Gifts"

...everything is dealt to us without fear or favor, after severe universal laws.

— REW —

If the man at the door have no shoes, you have not to consider whether you could procure him a paint-box.

— REW —

Rings and other jewels are not gifts, but apologies for gifts. The only gift is a portion of

From "Gifts"

thyself. Therefore the poet brings his poem;
the shepherd, his lamb; the farmer, corn.

— R E W —

He is a good man who can receive a gift well.

From "Nature"

The rounded world is fair to see,
Nine times folded in mystery:
Though baffled seers cannot impart
The secret of its laboring heart,
Throb thine with Nature's throbbing
   breast,
And all is clear from east to west.
Spirit that lurks each form within
Beckons to spirit of its kin;
Self-kindled every atom glows,
And hints the future which it owes.

— *REW* —

At the gates of the forest, the surprised man of
the world is forced to leave his city estimates of

great and small, wise and foolish. . . . Here is a sanctity which shames our religions, and reality which discredits our heroes.

— R *E* W —

We nestle in nature, and draw our living as parasites from her roots and grains, and we receive glances from the heavenly bodies, which call us to solitude and foretell the remotest future.

— R *E* W —

. . . he who knows what sweets and virtues are in the ground, the waters, the plants, the heavens and how to come at these enchantments,—is the rich and royal man.

— R *E* W —

Nature cannot be surprised in undress. Beauty breaks in everywhere.

The Sage from Concord

— R&W —

Nature is loved by what is best in us.

— R&W —

Motion or change and identity or rest are the first and second secrets of nature:—Motion and Rest. The whole code of her laws may be written on the thumbnail.

— R&W —

Things are so strictly related that according to the skill of the eye, from any one object the parts and properties of any other may be predicted. If we had eyes to see it, a bit of stone from the city wall would certify us of the necessity that man must exist, as readily as the city. That identity makes us all one.

— R&W —

From "Nature"

Nature, who made the mason, made the house.

— R E W —

Every known fact in natural science was divined by the presentiment of somebody, before it was actually verified.

— R E W —

Perhaps the discovery that wisdom has other tongues and ministers than we, that though we should hold our peace the truth would not the less be spoken, might check injuriously the flames of our zeal.

— R E W —

We live in a system of approximations. Every end is prospective of some other end, which is also temporary; a round and final success nowhere. We are encamped in nature, not domesticated.

— *REW* —

To the intelligent, nature converts itself into a vast promise, and will not be rashly explained. Her secret is untold.

— *REW* —

It appears that our actions are seconded and disposed to greater conclusions than we designed. We are escorted on every hand through life by spiritual agents, and a beneficent purpose lies in wait for us.

— *REW* —

The knowledge that we traverse the whole scale of being, from the center to the poles of nature, and have some stake in every possibility, lends that sublime luster to death, which

philosophy and religion have too outwardly
and literally striven to express in the popular
doctrine of the immortality of the soul. The
reality is more excellent than the report.

— *REW* —

Nature is the incarnation of a thought...The
world is mind precipitated.

— *REW* —

That power which does not respect quantity,
which makes the whole and the particle its
equal channel, delegates its smile to the morning, and distills its essence into every drop of
rain.

— *REW* —

Every moment instructs, and every object; for
wisdom is infused into every form.

— *REW* —

Beauty is the mark God sets upon virtue.
Every natural action is graceful. Every heroic
act is also decent. . . We are taught by great actions that the universe is the property of every
individual in it. Every rational creature has all
nature for his dowry and estate.

— R E W —

All good is eternally reproductive. The beauty
of nature re-forms itself in the mind, and not
for barren contemplation, but for new creation.

— R E W —

Truth, and goodness, and beauty are but dif-
ferent faces of the same All. But beauty in
nature is not ultimate. It is the herald of inward and eternal beauty. . . . It must stand as a
part, and not as yet the last or highest expression of the final cause of Nature.

From "Nominalist and Realist"

Wherever you go, a wit like your own has been before you, and has realized its thought. The Eleusinian mysteries, the Egyptian architecture, the Indian astronomy, the Greek sculpture, show that there have always been seeing and knowing men in the planet.

— ℛℰ𝒲 —

Proportion is almost impossible to human beings. There is no one who does not exaggerate.

— ℛℰ𝒲 —

As much as a man is a whole, so is he also a part; and it were partial not to see it.

The Sage from Concord

— REW —

The eye must not lose sight for a moment of the purpose.

— REW —

As long as any man exists, there is some need of him.

— REW —

Every man is wanted, and no man is wanted much.

— REW —

For rightly every man is a channel through which heaven floweth, and whilst I fancied I was criticizing him, I was censuring or rather terminating my own soul.

100

From "Nominalist and Realist"

— R𝓔W —

It is the secret of the world that all things subsist and do not die but only retire a little from sight and afterwards return again. Whatever does not concern us is concealed from us.

— R𝓔W —

Nothing is dead; men feign themselves dead, and endure mock funerals and mournful obituaries, and there they stand looking out of the window, sound and well, in some new and strange disguise.

— R𝓔W —

Love shows me the opulence of nature, by disclosing to me in my friend a hidden wealth, and I infer an equal depth of good in every other direction.

101

The Sage from Concord

— ℛℰ𝓌 —

No sentence will hold the whole truth.

— ℛℰ𝓌 —

We fancy men are individuals; so are pump-
kins; but every pumpkin in the field goes
through every point of pumpkin history.

From "Language"

The use of natural history is to give us aid in supernatural history; the use of the outer creation, to give us language for the beings and changes of the inward creation.

— *REW* —

It is not words only that are emblematic; it is things which are emblematic. Every natural fact is a symbol of some spiritual fact.

— *REW* —

The corruption of man is followed by the corruption of language.

103

The Sage from Concord

— RℰW —

...good writing and brilliant discourse are perpetual allegories. This imagery is spontaneous. It is the blending of experience with the present action of the mind. It is proper creation. It is the working of the Original Cause through the instruments he has already made.

— RℰW —

Have mountains, and waves, and skies, no significance but what we consciously give them when we employ them as emblems of our thoughts? The world is emblematic. Parts of speech are metaphors because the whole of nature is a metaphor of the human mind.

From "Plato;
or The Philosopher"

Philosophy is the account which the human mind gives to itself of the constitution of the world. Two cardinal facts lie forever at the base: the one, and the two. 1. Unity, or Identity; and 2. Variety . . . It is impossible to speak or think without embracing both.

— *R E W* —

The Same, the Same: friend and foe are of one stuff; the ploughman, the plough and the furrow are of one stuff; and the stuff is such and so much that the variations of form are unimportant.

— R&W —

The words *I* and *mine* constitute ignorance.

— R&W —

Nature is manifold. The unity absorbs, and melts or reduces. Nature opens and creates.

— R&W —

...there is a science of sciences—I call it Dialectic—which is the Intellect discriminating the false and the true. It rests on the observation of identity and diversity; for to judge is to unite to an object the notion which belongs to it.

— R&W —

I give you joy, O sons of man! that truth is altogether wholesome; that we have hope

106

to search out what might be the very self of everything. The misery of man is to be baulked of the sight of essence and to be stuffed with conjectures; but the supreme good is reality; the supreme beauty is reality; and all virtue and all felicity depend on this science of the real.

— *RᏉᎳ* —

There is no thought in any mind but it quickly tends to convert itself into a power and organizes a huge instrumentality of means.

— *RᏉᎳ* —

To these four sections, the four operations of the soul correspond: conjecture, faith, understanding, reason.

— *RᏉᎳ* —

107

...there is another, which is as much more beautiful than beauty as beauty is than chaos; namely, wisdom, which our wonderful organ of sight cannot reach unto, but which, could it be seen, would ravish us with its perfect reality.

— R℮W —

No power of genius has ever yet had the smallest success in explaining existence. The perfect enigma remains.

— R℮W —

The mind does not create what it perceives, any more than the eye creates the rose.

— R℮W —

Plato affirms the coincidence of science and virtue; for vice can never know itself and virtue, but virtue knows both itself and vice.

— R E W —

There is no lawless particle, and there is nothing casual in the action of the human mind.

The Sage from Concord

PAN

O what are heroes, prophets, men,
But pipes through which the breath of Pan
    doth blow
A momentary music. Being's tide
Swells hitherward, and myriads of forms
Live, robed with beauty, painted by the sun;
Their dust, pervaded by the nerves of God,
Throbs with an overmastering energy
Knowing and doing. Ebbs the tide, they lie
White hollow shells upon the desert shore,
But not the less the eternal wave rolls on
To animate new millions, and exhale
Races and planets, its enchanted foam.

From "Fate"

If you please to plant yourself on the side of
Fate, and say, Fate is all; then we say, a part
of Fate is the freedom of man.

— R.E.W —

The day of days, the great day of the feast of
life, is that in which the inward eye opens to
the Unity in things....This beatitude dips
from on high down on us and we see. It is not
in us so much as we are in it.

— R.E.W —

Fate is unpenetrated causes.

— ℛℰ𝒲 —

In the latest race, in man, every generosity, every new perception, the love and praise he extorts from his fellows, are certificates of advance out of fate into freedom.

— ℛℰ𝒲 —

The knot of nature is so well tied that nobody was ever cunning enough to find the two ends. Nature is intricate, overlapped, interweaved and endless. Christopher Wren said of the beautiful King's College chapel, that "if anybody would tell him where to lay the first stone, he would build such another." But where shall we find the first atom in the house of man.

— ℛℰ𝒲 —

A man's fortunes are the fruit of his character. A man's friends are his magnetisms.

From "Power"

There is not yet any inventory of a man's faculties, any more than a bible of his opinions. Who shall set a limit to the influence of a human being?

From "Wealth"

Nature arms each man with some faculty which enables him to do easily some feat impossible to any other, and thus makes him necessary to society.

— REW —

Nothing is beneath you if it is in the direction of your life...

From "Society and Solitude"

We pray to be conventional. But the wary Heaven takes care you shall not be, if there is anything good in you.

— R℮W —

Solitude is impracticable, and society fatal. We must keep our head in the one and our hands in the other. The conditions are met, if we keep our independence, yet do not lose our sympathy.

— R℮W —

From "Illusions"

There is no chance and no anarchy in the universe. All is system and gradation. Every god is there sitting in his sphere.

From "Culture"

A man is the prisoner of his power. A topical memory makes him an almanac; a talent for debate, a disputant; skill to get money makes him a miser, that is, a beggar.

— R E W —

Nature is reckless of the individual. When she has points to carry, she carries them.

— R E W —

A great part of courage is the courage of having done the thing before. And in all human action those faculties will be strong which are used.

116

From "Culture"

— R E W —

...there is in every constitution a certain solstice when the stars stand still in our inward firmament, and when there is required some foreign force, some diversion or alternative to prevent stagnation.

— R E W —

I suffer every day from the want of perception of beauty in people. They do not know the charm with which all moments and objects can be embellished, the charm of manners, of self-command, of benevolence.

— R E W —

A cheerful intelligent face is the end of culture, and success enough. For it indicates the purpose of nature and wisdom attained.

From "New England Reformers"

...God made yeast as well as dough, and loves fermentation just as dearly as he loves vegetation.

— R̃Ẽ W —

...there is no part of society or of life better than any other part. All our things are right and wrong together.

— R̃Ẽ W —

Men will live and communicate, and plow, and reap, and govern, as by added ethereal power, when once they are united....But this

118

union must be inward and not one of the covenants....The union must be ideal in actual individualism.

— ℛℰ𝒲 —

Life must be lived on a higher plane. We must go up to a higher platform, to which we are always invited to ascend; there the whole aspect of things changes.

— ℛℰ𝒲 —

The soul lets no man go without some visitations and holy-days of a divine presence.

— ℛℰ𝒲 —

Nothing shall warp me from the belief that every man is a lover of truth.

— ℛℰ𝒲 —

119

There is a power over and behind us, and we are the channels of its communication. This open channel to the highest life is the first and last reality, so subtle, so quiet, yet so tenacious, that although I have never expressed truth, and although I have never heard the expression of it from any other, I know that the whole truth is here for me.

— *REW* —

The life of man is the true romance, which, when it is valiantly conducted, will yield the imagination a higher joy than any fiction.

— *REW* —

It is so wonderful to our neurologists that a man can see without his eyes, that it does not occur to them that it is just as wonderful that he should see with them; and that is ever the difference between the wise and the unwise; the latter wonders at what is unusual, the wise man wonders at the usual.

From "Representative Men"

A man is a center for nature, running out threads of relation through everything, fluid and solid, material and elemental...every organ, function, acid, crystal, grain of dust, has its relation to the brain. It waits long, but its turn comes. Each plant has its parasite, and each created thing its lover and poet.

— *REW* —

Something is wanting in science, until it has been humanized....Each material thing has its celestial side.

— *REW* —

Rotation is the law of nature.

121

— R&W —

There needs but one wise man in a company, and all are wise, so rapid is the contagion.

— R&W —

There is something deceptive about the inter-course of minds. The boundaries are invisible, but they are never crossed. There is such good will to impart, and such good will to receive, that each threatens to become the other; but the law of individuality collects its secret strength; you are you and I am I, and so we remain.

From "The American Scholar"

It is one of those fables, which, out of an unknown antiquity, convey an unlooked-for wisdom, that the gods, in the beginning, divided Man into men, that he might be more helpful to himself; just as the hand was divided into fingers, the better to answer its end. The old fable covers a doctrine ever new and sublime; that there is One Man,—present to all particular men only partially, or through one faculty; and that you must take the whole society to find the whole man.

— REW —

[Man] learns that in going down into the secrets of his own mind, he has descended into the secrets of all minds.

— R E W —

It is one light which beams out of a thousand stars. It is one soul which animates all men.

— R E W —

Man is surprised to find that things near are not less beautiful and wondrous than things remote. The near explains the far. The drop is a small ocean. A man is related to all nature.

— R E W —

There is never a beginning, there is never an end, to the inexplicable continuity of this web of God, but always circular power returning to itself.

From "The American Scholar"

— R E W —

In self-trust all the virtues are compre-
hended....For this self-trust the reason is
deeper than can be fathomed—darker than
can be enlightened.

— R E W —

Nature is the opposite of the soul, answering to
it part for part. One is seal, and one is print.
Its beauty is the beauty of [our] own mind. Its
laws are the laws of [our] own mind.

— R E W —

So much of nature as [a person] is ignorant of,
so much of his own mind does he not yet pos-
sess. And, in fine, the ancient precept, "Know
thyself," and the modern precept, "Study
nature," become at last one maxim.

The Sage from Concord

— ℛℰ𝒲 —

I embrace the common, I explore and sit at the feet of the familiar, the low. Give me insight into today, and you may have the antique and future worlds.

Terminus

TERMINUS

As the bird trims her to the gale,
I trim myself to the storm of time,
I man the rudder, reef the sail,
Obey the voice at eve obeyed at prime:
"Lowly faithful, banish fear,
Right onward drive unharmed;
The port, well worth the cruise, is near,
And every wave is charmed."

*This book is one of the Quest Miniature
Series, a special imprint of the Theosophical
Publishing House. Other Quest Miniatures are:*

At the Feet of the Master *by Alcyone*
The Buddhist Catechism *by Henry Steel Olcott*
Circle of Wisdom *by Helena Petrovna Blavatsky*
An Experience of Enlightenment *by Flora Courtois*
Finding Deep Joy *by Robert Ellwood*
Finding the Quiiet Mind *by Robert Ellwood*
Fragments *by C. Jinarajadasa*
Freedom Through the Balisier *by Cyril H. Boynes*
From the Outer Court to the Inner Sanctum
                              by Annie Besant
Gifts of the Lotus *Comp. by Virginia Hanson*
Hymn of Jesus *by G. R. S. Mead*
Light on the Path *by Mabel Collins*
Natural Man *by Henry David Thoreau*
Reflective Meditation *by Kay Mouradian*
The Song Celestial *by Sir Edwin Arnold*
Tao *by Charles H. Mackintosh*
Thoughts for Aspirants *by N. Sri Ram*
Trust Yourself to Life *by Clara Codd*
Voice of the Silence *by Helena Petrovna Blavatsky*
When the Sun Moves Northward *by Mabel Collins*

Available from:
QUEST BOOKS
306 West Geneva Road
Wheaton, Illinois 60187